Copyright © 2021.

All rights reserved. No part of this publication may be reproduced, distributed, or transmitted in any form or by any means, including photocopying, recording, or other electronic or mechanical methods, without the prior written permission of the publisher, except in the case of brief quotations embodied in critical reviews and certain other noncommercial uses permitted by copyright law. For permission requests, write to the author at gotmixinfo@gmail.com.

ISBN:978-163877447-1
Printed by Lulu Press, Inc, in the United States of America.

First printing edition 2021.

SPE CAMP
Road To Greatness
FIRST EDITION

BY: TAIWAN MIXON

DEDICATIONS

This book is dedicated to parents and athletes that seek to follow the stories of athletes that went from high school to college to professional by way of the SPE Elite National Camp platform.

ACKNOWLEDGMENTS

On behalf of SPE Elite National Camp board of directors, we would like to thank the parents, coaches, media, friends, family, my pastor, my leader, all of the players, colleges and scouts.

We wish to thank you for taking the time to visit our camp and experience the value of our platform in helping athlete's accomplish their goals. Our entire staff are always thrilled to work with the players every year. We hope that you enjoyed your time with us and that your experience empowered you and your child in their life and career.

ABOUT SPE

SPE Elite National Camp offers a unique football camp experience for aspiring college prospects primarily for high school freshmen, sophomores and juniors. The emphasis here is on developing the student-athlete in preparation for the recruitment process.

While the combines offer a platform for the student-athlete to showcase and enhance his abilities on the field and in the training room, academics are also stressed. SPE stands for speed, power, and exposure in which is what every player needs in the recruiting process.

SPE CAMP

Road To Greatness
FIRST EDITION

"Live Your Life One Day At A Time."

—Wiseman

Jeffrey Simmons

DT Mississippi St./NFL

Jeffrey Simmons was the #1 player in high school in the state of Mississippi. He is an All-American who was one of the best defensive players in the nation. He decided to drive down to the camp from Mississippi which is a 8 hour drive to Houston, Texas. He got in line at the camp for registration check in and once he got to the front, he saw the big trophy and stated, "That's mine... I'm taking that trophy back to Mississippi." The Director told the young man, "hey you know this camp is only for high school players right?" Simmons replied, "I'm a junior sir."

He checked in and went to the media booth where Rivals and Gotmix news was waiting to interview him. During the camp, Simmons was putting on a show at defensive line and also offensive line. He was doing so well that he went up against former NFL OL Tony Ugoh of the Indianapolis Colts during 1vs1. He scored a victory against Mr. Ugoh which ultimately won him the MVP of the entire camp. He ended playing in the All-American Bowl high school all star game, and ended up going to Mississippi State University (MSU) on a scholarship. He was featured in MSU history during his three years with the program. The Titans selected Jeffery Simmons with the 19th overall pick in the 2019 NFL Draft.

Jerry Jeudy
WR Alabama/NFL

Jerry Jeudy got off the plane at Bush Continental. The stud WR from Florida came to the SPE Elite Camp and showed off some fancy footwork throughout the day. He kept defensive backs twisting and turning throughout the day as he kept them guessing which way he would turn next.

He was able to shake loose from defenders throughout the day and his ability to change direction at the drop of a hat was easy to spot.
A rookie wide receiver who appeared in 42 games (27 starts) at the University of Alabama, totaling 159 receptions for 2,742 yards (17.2 avg.) with 26 touchdowns during his collegiate career (2017-19). Biletnikoff Award (nation's top WR) recipient following his sophomore season after posting 68 receptions for 1,315 yards (19.3 avg.) with 14 touchdowns. He was selected by the Denver Broncos in the first round 15th overall.

Bravvion Roy
DT Baylor/NFL

Bravvion Roy, from Spring High School in Houston, Texas, came to the SPE Elite Camp as a 3-star prospect. The 6'2 ,300-pounder was dominant in 1vs1's while at the camp and was selected as one of the top DL players at the camp. He played four seasons at Baylor under Matt Rhule. He tallied 133 tackles, 7.5 sacks and 19.0 tackles for loss in his career. Bravvion Earned first team All-Big 12 honors in 2019, tallying career highs with 5.5 sacks and 13.0 tackles for loss.

Roy also produced one forced fumble, seven QB hurries, one blocked kick and 61 total tackles. Had five tackles with one sack in the Sugar Bowl against Georgia. Also had five tackles including 1.5 for a loss in Big 12 title game against Oklahoma in junior season, had 34 tackles and 1.5 sacks. Bravvion Roy was selected by the Carolina Panthers in the sixth round.

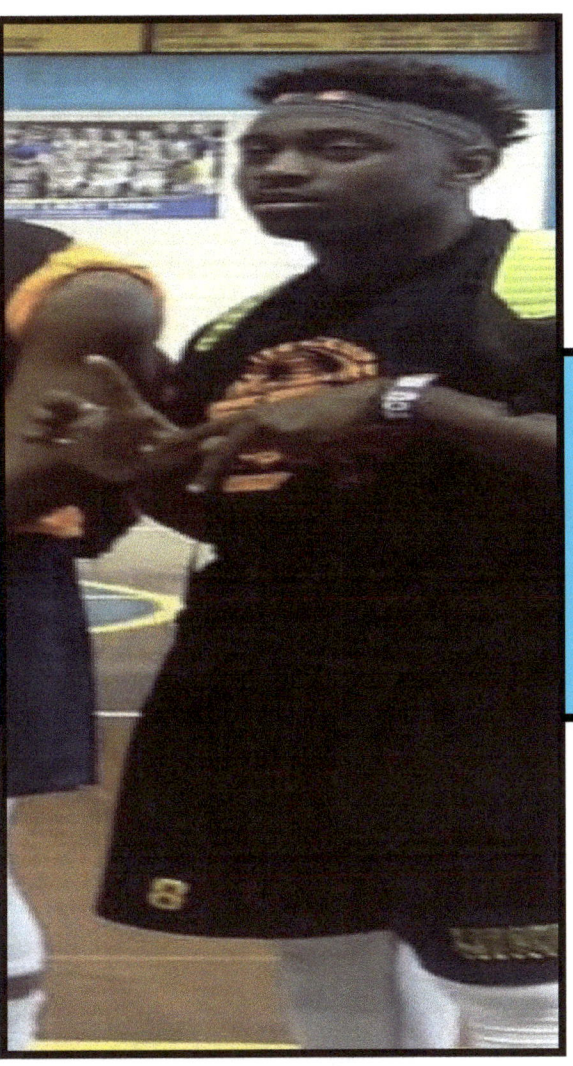

Patrick Queen LB
LSU/NFL

Patrick Queen was a delight when he was at the SPE Elite Camp. Patrick was a running back in high school in Louisiana. When he came to the SPE Camp, he signed up as a linebacker because he said that the college that he wanted to go to, LSU, wanted to try him out at the linebacker position. He said he wanted to perfect his craft. Patrick emerged as one of LSU's top defenders in 2019. He played the best football of his LSU career down the stretch, earning defensive MVP honors in the win over Clemson in the national championship game. The versatile linebacker mentored under All-American and Butkus Award winner, Devin White a year ago. He was placed in the lineup after their star linebacker was suspended. He capped off his career playing in 41 games, and starting 16 times. With 131 career tackles along with 17.5 tackles for loss and 4 sacks he opted to forgo final season at LSU and entered into the 2020 NFL Draft.

Ed Oliver
DT Houston/NFL

Ed Oliver came to SPE Elite National Camp as one of the best players in the nation. Not only was the camp held at his high school but he also wanted people to know why he committed to the home town school in his city Houston University. Oliver became the first three-time All-American in the history of the program and also became the first player in Houston history to earn first-team all-conference honors in three different years.

Oliver was the Outland Trophy winner and Nagurski finalist, Oliver led the nation with a career average of 1.56 tackles for loss per game, totaling 39.5 tackles for loss in only 25 games. Oliver was labeled a Five-star recruit by ESPN, Rivals, Scout and 247Sports. No. 1 defensive tackle in the state of Texas by Scout. He was named the Defensive MVP in the 2016 Under Armour All-America Game. He chose Houston over Alabama, Baylor, LSU, Mississippi, Notre Dame, Oklahoma, Texas and Texas A&M among others coached by Matt Meekins at Westfield HS. The Buffalo Bills select Houston defensive tackle Ed Oliver No. 9 in Round 1 of the 2019 NFL Draft.

Jack Jones
WR/DB USC/ASU

Jack Jones, from Long Beach Poly HS in California, was flat awesome at the camp, He walked out the camp MVP after playing WR and DB at a high level. Jones, now at ASU, made an instant impact in Tempe, collecting 45 tackles, 13 pass breakups, three interceptions, and a forced fumble. While at USC, Jones collected 40 total tackles, a team-leading four interceptions, as well as eight pass breakups during a productive sophomore season. Collected 40 total tackles, a team-leading four interceptions, as well as eight pass breakups during a productive sophomore season. Jones dominated both sides of the ball and played on special teams at Long Beach Poly High School. He was a part of the USA Today All-California first team, and was one of the country's most highly sought-after prospects.

Deriq King QB
UH/UM

Mr. King has always competed wherever he goes. King ,a QB from Houston, now the Miami Hurricanes starting QB in 2020. While King was at UH he delivered a dominant career at University of Houston, finishing with 78 total touchdowns (50 passing, 28 rushing), 4,925 passing yards and 1,421 rushing yards despite starting just 22 games. Totaled 6,346 yards of offense (181.3 per game). Set The American Athletic Conference touchdown season record with 50 despite missing the last 2.5 games with an injury in 2018. He led the nation in points responsible for per game with an average of 27.5, four points ahead of the No 2 spot shared by Heisman finalists Kyler Murray and Dwayne Haskins during prolific junior season.

King had a rushing touchdown in all 11 games in 2018 and one of only three QBs in FBS history with at least 35 passing TDs and 13 rushing TDs . King was the 2018 Maxwell Award semifinalist and Earl Campbell Award finalist. At Manvel High School, King was a four-star recruit by ESPN and member of ESPN300, ranked No. 202 overall. He went on to be named district 22-6A MVP as a senior, and named first team All-Greater Houston Elite 11 semifinalist. King has a career with over 10,000 career passing yards and 3,000 career rushing yards.

Gary Haynes
WR ULL/TSU

Mr. Haynes put on a clinic at SPE Camp on offense and defense which got him the camp MVP. Gary Haynes was a three-star recruit by Scout.com and Rivals.com and rated as the No. 28 wide receiver in the state of Texas and No. 30 in the Texas Midland. He was ranked as the No.141 wide receiver in the nation and No. 136 recruit in Texas by 247sports.com.

He caught 67 passes for 1,047 yards and 12 touchdowns as a senior and was named a First-Team All-District 22-6A selection. He helped lead Manvel HS to a 13-1 record, the District 22-6A title and an appearance in the Class 6A-Division II regional finals and was named MVP of the Nike Football Training Camp in Houston. Haynes 11th grade year he caught 52 passes for 879 yards and 13 TDs.

Hunter Hagdorn
WR Dartmouth

Hunter came to the SPE Camp and ended up being the top WR at the camp. Hunter had a lot of offers but decided on IVY league because of the education opportunity. He finished his career fourth at Dartmouth with 160 receptions, tied for fifth with 15 touchdown catches and sixth with 2,015 receiving yards.

While he was in high school, he was a three-time letterman for Kirk Martin at Manvel. The two-star receiver who caught 36 passes for 595 yards and 10 touchdowns as a senior averaged 16.5 yards per reception and helped his team go 39-5 over last four years, winning district title each time. He finished his high school career with 62 grabs for 992 yards captained team as a senior. Hagdorn was listed on Vype Top 100 Houston in the final season and selected for an all-district first team. He was also the Touchdown Club of Houston Scholar-Athlete of the Year as a senior.

(TX) James Kohlschmidt
LB Colorado School of Mines

James came to the SPE Elite National Camp and was the top linebacker. He is a two-year letter winner from Cy Fair High School in Houston, Texas. He was a unanimous first team all-district selection in 2013 and 2014 and twice led the team to the third round of state playoffs, winning the district championship in 2013. While at Colorado School of Mines he was a captain, Iron Digger Award winner, Honorable Mention All-RMAC, and started 12 times in 13 appearances as inside linebacker. James was fourth on the team in total tackles with 53, had 5.5 tackles for loss with a sack and three hurries. His top game was a 10-tackle, 1.0-TFL performance against Dixie State. He had six stops in the NCAA First Round against Sioux Falls. Also he had six tackles including five solo stops at Chadron State.

(TX) Jacoby Simpson
LB TCU/ECU

Jacoby Simpson a linebacker that showed up to the camp from Houston, Texas. He lined up on running backs during 1v1 and then went over and lined up on wide receivers. Jacoby was a four-year all-district selection and an Associated Press Class 6A All-State (honorable mention) choice as a senior at Aldine-MacArthur. He tallied 116 tackles (76 solo), 19.0 TFLs, eight sacks, three forced fumbles and two interceptions during senior season in 2017 . Jacobt chose TCU over lots of schools right out of high school, and jumped in the transfer portal and committed to East Carolina on September 4, 2020.

(CA) Elijah Hicks
DB Cal/NFL

Elijah finished his senior campaign with 1001 all-purpose yards and a total of 10 touchdowns with five receiving, three on punt returns including a 96-yarder, one kick return and one interception return. Recorded 31 receptions for 483 yards and five touchdown catches as a senior, while adding 40 tackles, 1.0 tackle for loss (-6 yards) and five interceptions that he returned 15 yards on defense.

Elijah has played in all 42 games possible with 34 starts over the last four seasons since his arrival in January of 2017 and posted career totals of 141 tackles, 9.0 tackles for loss (-25 yards), 2.0 sacks (-7 yards), two interceptions that he returned for a combined 64 yards and one touchdown, 12 pass breakups, 14 passes defended and two forced fumbles.

(CA) Eli Ricks
DB LSU

Eli played at IMG Academy in Bradenton, Florida after transferring from Mater Dei High School in Santa Ana, Calif. He was ranked as the No. 1 overall prospect in the state of Florida by 247Sporsts, MaxPreps and Rivals. Eli was listed as a five-star cornerback by 247Sports and by Rivals, rated a four-star cornerback and ranked 29th by ESPN 300. He played in 10 games as a senior, tallying 14 solo tackles and three interceptions. Ranked the No. 1 cornerback out of Florida by 247Sports, MaxPreps and Rivals. Eli won back-to-back national championships at Mater Dei High School in Santa Ana, Calif. He ranked the No. 7 player by Chosen 25 All-USA First Team Defensive Player in 2018. In 10 games, seven of which were starts, Ricks had 20 tackles and nine passes defended. He returned two of his interceptions for touchdowns, the second coming in LSU's win over sixth-ranked Florida. His other interception return for a touchdown came in the win over South Carolina. Ricks also earned Freshman All-SEC honors and was named third team All-American by the Associated Press. Ricks becomes the third LSU defensive back to earn FWAA Freshman All-America honors.

(LA) TJ Finley
QB LSU

The top quarterback in the state of Louisiana, in 2019 TJ prepped at Ponchatoula High School in Ponchatoula, Louisiana. He was rated a three-star pro-style quarterback by 247Sports and Rivals . TJ served as a three-year starter for Ponchatoula High Schooland accounted for 72 touchdowns during his high school career (58 passing, 14 rushing). He completed a career-high 168 passes as a senior for 2,738 yards to go along with 21 touchdowns. He rushed for eight touchdowns as a senior. Amassed 28 touchdowns during his junior season, 23 through the air and five on the ground. TJ passed for 2,736 yards in 2018.

Overall, TJ accumulated a total of 7,357 yards through his three years at quarterback coached by Hank Tierney. Mr. Finley had a nice freshman year at LSU. He threw for 941 yards and 5 TDs and 5 Ints while completing 57 percent of his passes.

(CA) DJ Uiagalelei
QB Clemson

DJ was the top QB at the camp. In high school, DJ was the top quarterback in the nation according to Rivals.com and PrepStar named him a USA Today All-American after leading his team to No. 1 ranking by MaxPreps and USA Today after guiding them to a 7A state championship in California. He threw for 10,496 yards in his high school career and had 127 career touchdowns against just 11 interceptions. He completed 585-of-871 passes for a 66 percent completion mark . DJ averaged 18 yards per completion and also rushed for 1,103 yards and 18 touchdowns in his career, a 6.1 yard-per-carry average.

Dj is a cannon-armed passer who enters 2021 following an impressive true freshman campaign in which he completed 78-of-117 passes for 914 yards with five touchdowns and no interceptions in 235 snaps over 10 games (two starts) as a true freshman in 2020. He also enters 2021 credited with 28 carries for 60 yards and four rushing touchdowns.

(TX) John Holcombe
QB Kansas St./FAU

Mr. Holcombe came to the SPE Elite National Camp and put on a passing clinic by showing off his strong arm and mobility in the pocket to the point where he won the top QB award. In high school, he played at Summer Creek High School under head coach Brian Ford. John was rated the 13th-best dual-threat quarterback in the Class of 2018 by 247Sports, while he was ranked 28th by Rivals and 33rd by ESPN. He was viewed as the fifth-best dual-threat quarterback in the state of Texas by Lone Star Prospects.

John was named the UIL District 21-6A Offensive MVP in 2017 after throwing for 2,369 yards and 22 touchdowns. He also rushed for 551 yards and another nine scores during senior season. He earned VYPE Magazine All-Houston honors and helped the Bulldogs advance to the area round of the 6A state playoffs. John was named a second team all-district performer as a junior in 2016. He also participated in track and field.

(LA) Jontre Kirklin
WR LSU

Mr. Kirklin came to the SPE Camp as a quarterback and ended up asking if he could play WR at the camp as well. He played the WR position that day and won one of the top WR awards, a few days later LSU gave him an offer and he commited. In high school, he made the transition from dual-threat quarterback to the secondary in college. Swift and elusive with exceptional running ability, Jontre demonstrates impressive instincts and has shown the ability to properly diagnose plays as a defender due to his offensive background. He was a unanimous 3-star prospect by Scout, ESPN, Rivals and 247 Sports . Rated as the No. 30 recruit in Louisiana . Jontre was ranked the No. 3 athlete in Louisiana by Scout and helped lead the Lutcher Bulldogs to repeat as Class 3A state champions finishing his career with 147 touchdowns, over 7,500 yards passing and 3,000 rushing yards.

(FL) Jacquez Jones
WR Tennesse/EKU

The Florida product came to SPE Elite National Camp and walked away as the top WR. He is currently at EKU and played in all nine games. He started five times and led the team with 40 receptions and was second with 578 receiving yards and caught four touchdown passes at an average of 64.2 receiving yards per game. Jacquez averaged 4.4 receptions per game and 14.4 yards per reception after the fall season. He was ranked fourth in the nation in receiving yards, sixth in receiving touchdowns, eighth in receptions per game. He had three receptions and three touchdowns vs The Citadel. He posted a season-best 136 yards on six catches in a win over No. 11 Central Arkansas. As a senior, he caught 57 passes for 1,004 yards and 10 touchdowns while rushing for 244 yards and four TDs on 23 carries.

(CA) Drake Metcalf
OL Stanford

Drake came to SPE Elite Camp and walked away with the top lineman award. He played at St. John Bosco High School for head coach Jason Negro. He is a Four-star recruit by both Rivals and PrepStar, where he's ranked No. 324 nationally. He was a consensus top 40 player from California – ranked No. 32 by Rivals, No. 37 by PrepStar and No. 39 by 247Sports. Drake ranked as a top 10 center by Rivals (No. 5), PrepStar (No. 5) and 247Sports (No. 8). He played in the 2020 Polynesian Bowl. He was a two-time MaxPreps All-American (2018-19) All-state first team (2019). He was a team captain (2019) and All-CIFSS first team (2018) All-area (2018). He led his team to 2019 CIF Open Division State Championship and No. 1 national ranking. He helped his team to 2018 Trinity League Championship Member of 2016 D1 State Champions and was CIFSS Champions Four-time recipient of the Scholar-Athlete Award also earning a spot on the Principal's Honor Roll all four years. He was named Student of the Year for AP U.S. History as a junior and also Freshman Entrepreneur of the Year.

(CA) Xamarion Gordon
USC

Mr. Gordon won the top safety award at the SPE Elite National Camp. Xamarion is versatile and rangy with the ability to play multiple positions in college. He plays safety at the HS level but has the frame to easily bulk up into an outside backer in college. He is one of the more physical players in the region who plays with a head hunter mentality. Xamarion can fly off the hash and is a big hitter in run support and is an intimidating presence in the passing game as well. He has improved in coverage and he plays very hard and is a highly competitive player with natural leadership ability.

(CA) Bryce Young
QB Alabama

Bryce Young is a 5-11, 183-pound Dual-Threat Quarterback from Los Angeles, CA who won the top QB award at SPE Elite National Camp. In 2019, he was an All-American Bowl Player of the Year, Gatorade Player of the Year in California, High School Quarterback of the Year by the National Quarterback Club, Maxwell Offensive Player of the Year, MaxPreps Player of the Year (shared with fellow five-star quarterback DJ Uiagalelei), among many other awards. He finished his high school career with 13,250 passing yards and 152 passing touchdowns to go along with 1,084 rushing yards and 26 more scores and accounted for 178 total touchdowns. During his first season, he went 13-of-22 passing for 156 yards and a touchdown.

(FL) Caleb Ward
WR Florida St.

Caleb was the Mind of an Athlete award Winner at the SPE Elite National Camp. He is an athletic wide receiver with tremendous separation skills dual-sport athlete in high school and also ran track as a senior. He reached the Florida 3A track and field championships in the triple jump. He is the son of FSU Hall of Famer and Heisman Trophy-winning quarterback Charlie Ward.

(CA) Na'im Rodman
DL Colorado

Na'im Rodman was the top DL at the SPE Elite National Camp. A 3-star prospect by the major recruiting services, 247Sports ranked him as the No. 59 defensive tackle in the nation and No. 108 player out of California under coach Jason Negro. At St. John Bosco, he helped the team compile a 37-6 record in his three years there and was named First-Team All-Trinity League as a senior when he had 59 tackles including 13 for a loss and three sacks helping St. John Bosco to a 13-1 record, a CIF Championship and No. 2 national ranking according to MaxPreps. During his junior season the team was 12-3 and he had 30 tackles including four for a loss and 2.5 sacks. During his sophomore season, the team compiled a 12-2 record . He also played rugby for one season and a flanker. He played in all 12 games and started two along the defensive line as a true freshman. His two starts came against Arizona and Washington. He finished the season playing 314 total snaps with 11 tackles.

(TX) Joshua Eaton
DB Oklahoma

In high school, Joshua played at Aldine MacArthur in Houston, Texas. The four-star recruit by 247Sports, ESPN and Rivals rated as the country's No. 438 recruit by 247Sports ranked as the No. 25 cornerback in the class by ESPN, No. 31 by Rivals and No. 33 by 247Sports ranked the No. 44 recruit in the state of Texas by Rivals, No. 53 by ESPN and No. 57 by 247Sports chose OU over Georgia, LSU, Texas and others.

In his freshman year, he played in five games and made four tackles notched one solo tackle at Texas Tech (10/31) and vs. Kansas (11/7) made one assisted tackle vs. Missouri State (9/12) and against No. 22 Texas (10/10).

(LA) Donald Clay
DB SMU

Donald Clay was SPE Elite National Camp top DB & Top Freshman award winner when he came to the camp. In high school, the three-star recruit by 247sports.com and Rivals.com was a All-state selection. Mr. Clay registered 59 tackles and three interceptions for 100 yards in 2018. He also had 94 kickoff return yards, 22 punt return yards and 225 all-purpose yards. His team went 13-0 and won the LHSAA Division I State Championship. Donald had offers from Memphis, Temple, Arizona State, Indiana, Kentucky, Virginia and others

In his second year, he played in all 10 games and registered 36 tackles (31 solo), including one for loss with three PBUs. In his first year, he redshirted and made the American Athletic Conference All-Academic Team. He finished the season playing 314 total snaps with 11 tackles.

(CA) Matayo Uiagalelei
(TE) St. John Bosco

Matayo was a freshman when he first came to the SPE Elite National Camp down in Louisiana. His brother, DJ Uiagalelei, is the starting QB at Clemson University, and was the top QB award winner at the camp. His little brother Matayo put on one of the best performances ever at the camp. He is one of the best athletes if not the best in class of '23. He did 1v1 vs offensive linemen and vs defensive backs. In both cases, he dominated upperclassmen. He looks to have a great year at St. John Bosco. He put on some nice weight and muscle while training at Winner Circle Academy.

(TX) Dematrius Davis
QB Auburn

Outstanding dual-threat quarterback who has led North Shore High to an 11-0 record and district and bi-district titles thus far in 2020. His career total yards is over 13,000. In 2020 he had 2,453 yards passing with 30 TD and 529 yards rushing with 14 scores as a senior for Coach Jon Kay. During his junior year, he led North Shore to a 15-1 record and second straight state championship.

Dematrius was district 21-6A MVP as a sophomore as the 16-0 Mustangs won the Texas 6A D-I state title. He was the MaxPreps sophomore of the year and ESPN rates him No. 4 dual-threat recruit nationally. He is a top 12 player at his position nationally by Rivals, 24/7, PrepStar among top 40 prospects in Texas. He is also a track and field letterman.

(TX) Shadrick Banks
WR Texas A&M

Mr. Banks went to North Shore in Houston Texas and played for coach John Kay. Stoutly-built receiver with the look of a running back or off-ball linebacker who excels as an open-field playmaker. He has a requisite height with mass typically associated with other positions. Shadrick ombines run strength with burst and good top-end play speed. He was fully healthy as a sophomore and a senior and amassed terrific production both seasons for elite North Shore squad. He is consistent and sometimes dominant against very good high school competition. He is a big-play machine and shows above average body control in contested situations and strength to win the ball over defenders. He has improved short-area quickness and elusiveness over the course of high school career. Not only an over-the-top threat but a dangerous run-after-catch option in the screen and short-to-intermediate games. Flat-out football player with big-play punch

(CA) Darion Green Warren
DB Michigan

In high school, for his senior year he attended Narbonne (2019) High School coached by Joe Aguirre. He played his high school career at Santa Ana Mater Dei and was on both state championship teams. During his sophomore and junior year before transferring to Narbonne as a senior, he was putting up numbers.

Darion registered 16 tackles, six of which were tackles for loss, and eight pass breakups As a senior, he recorded 26 tackles, 2.5 tackles for loss, three interceptions and six pass breakups. As a junior, he Made 29 stops, 1.0 TFLs, two interceptions and four PBUs. During his sophomore season, 247Sports Composite Rank he was 14th-best DB prospect. and a four-star recruit according to 247Sports.

(CA) Merlin Robertson
LB ASU

At SPE Elite National Camp, Merlin was the Top linebacker . In high school, he was a consensus four-star prospect among all major recruiting services. Tabbed as the No. 8 outside linebacker in the country by 24/7, the No. 11 linebacker by Rivals, and the No. 5 inside linebacker by ESPN. He was a four-year starter at Junipero Serra High School. Totaled 377 tackles, 54 tackles for loss, 19.5 sacks and eight forced fumbles during his varsity career.

Merlin had a huge senior season, totaling 126 tackles, 16 tackles for loss, seven sacks and two interceptions. His sophomore year at ASU he led the Sun Devils with three fumbles forced in 2019 and was third on the team with 72 tackles, adding 5 TFL and an interception. Led the team in tackles (77), tackles for loss (8.5) and sacks (5.0) and added an interception, two breakups, a fumble forced and a fumble recovered.

(LA) Tywan Francis
DB Colorado St.

He was the top DB at SPE Elite National Camp. As a junior, he had 51 tackles, three interceptions, 16 pass breakups, three forced fumbles, three recovered fumbles and a TD Tywan earned Defensive Most Valuable Player honors in his district and earned all-state honors in 2018. He helped lead his team to a 5A state title in Louisiana in 2016. He served as team captain during his senior season and maintained Honor Roll status as a junior and senior. Tywan selected CSU over 10 reported offers including Troy, Arkansas State and Louisiana Tech, while receiving interest from LSU, Arkansas and Mississippi State Parents are Arnold Barnes and Laura Perkins-Barnes. His older brother, Erskine, played football at Fort Scott C.C. and transferred to Austin Peay before the 2018 season.

(LA) Solomon Lewis
WR LA Tech

Was one of the top WR at SPE Elite Camp. He was rated as a three-star wide receiver by 247Sports.com. Named MaxPreps 2020 preseason All-Louisiana second team. Lewis helped lead the team an undefeated 10-1 season in 2020 and averaged 74.4 receiving yards per game as a senior.

He recorded 744 receiving yards on 43 receptions for 11 touchdowns in 2020. He totaled 1,449 receiving yards on 95 receptions for 19 touchdowns during his high school career. Lewis was named 2020 LSWA Class 3A all-state as a kick returner. He was coached by Erick Franklin and chose Louisiana Tech over offers from schools such as Fresno State, Houston, Miami (Fla.) and Texas Tech.

(LA) Freddie Mango
DB Grambling

Mango has impressive size for a high school athlete. He stands at a gargantuan 6'0 tall, and weighs in at concrete 194lbs. At this size, most would deem him unable to carry such a colossal weight, but even with his build, Mango runs an impressive 4.54 in the 40 yard dash.

He has sprinters speed, combined with ideal size, which makes him a terror on the offensive side of the ball. Along with size, Freddie has mammoth like strength and strives for physicality. When Freddie Mango touches the ball, all defenders should be put on notice.

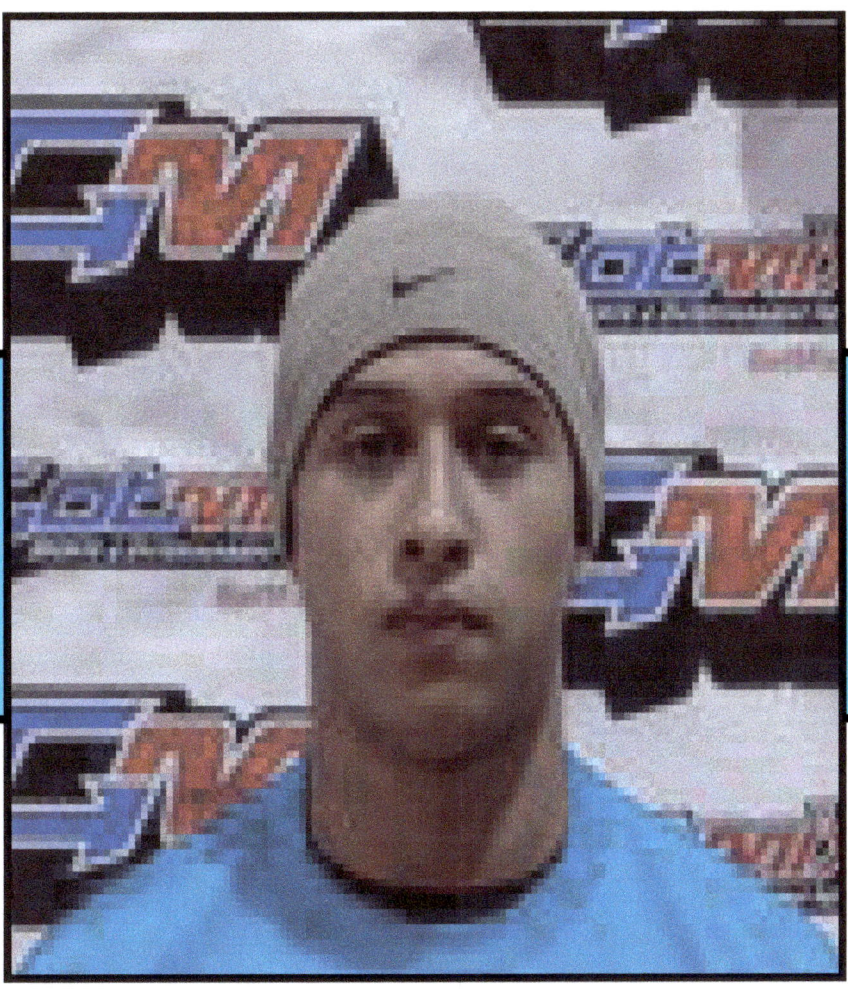

(CA) Titus Toler
DB Wisconsin

Titus is a three-star recruit by 247 Sports, ESPN and Rivals. He helped lead St. John Bosco (13-1) to CIF Southern Section Division 1 title game as a senior, recording 68 tackles, 4 interceptions and a fumble return touchdown. Titus also lettered in track and field and was coached by Jason Negro.

(TX) Cam Arnold
QB SFA

Lettered at Cy-Fair High School in Cypress, Texas, Cam led the Bobcats to their first ever state championship as a senior in 2017 . He went 15-0 as the starting quarterback and claimed the Class 6A Division II title, going 17-of-24 for 158 yards and two touchdowns in a semifinal upset to reach the state championship game. Cam threw for 2,012 yards and accounted for 26 touchdowns as a senior .

He collected 4,075 yards and 46 touchdowns in his prep career and was named first-team all-district and academic all-state. He tabbed All-Greater Houston in 2017. Cam was one of the top 50 pro-style quarterbacks in the nation by 247Sports.com He was named a Houston Chronicle Top-100 and finished his prep career 24-5 as a starter. Rated as a three star recruit by 247Sports.com and Rivals.com. His father, Jim, was an offensive lineman at LSU (1986-91).

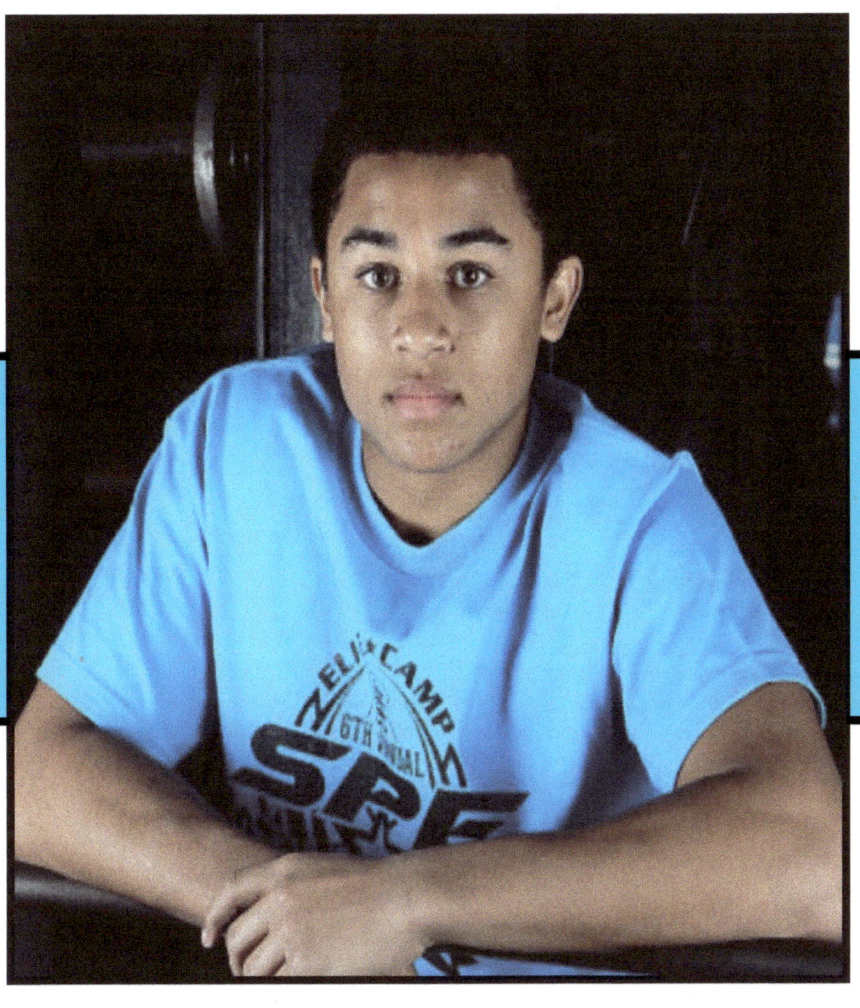

(CA) Trent McDuffie
DB Washington

Trent spent three years on the varsity at St. John Bosco as a senior and led St. John Bosco to a 13-1 overall record and advanced to the championship game of the CIF Southern Section Division 1 playoffs in 2018. He returned a blocked punt for a TD in the title game and finished the year ranked No. 3 in the nation by USA Today. He was named to USA Today's All-California second team following his senior season. His senior year he had 50 tackles, two picks and three fumble recoveries. Trent played for coach Jason Negro at Bosco.

Trent was named to the All-Pac-12 second team and was also named to Pro Football Focus' All-Pac-12 first team, and to the AP and Phil Steele second team and started every game of the 2020 season.

In 2019, he played in all 13 games, starting the last 11 of them named second-team Freshman All-America by ProFootballFocus.com. He also was a honorable mention Pac-12 Freshman Defensive Player of the Year and Pro Football Focus All-Pac-12 second team .

(NY) Armon Bethea
OL ASU

SPE Elite Camp Alumni All-American came from NY to the camp. The giant offensive line prospect with massive potential plays with an edge and mentality necessary for the role. He is a versatile athlete with the ability to play guard or tackle. He is a dominant force at the line of scrimmage, imposing his will on opponents. He finishes his blocks to ensure extra yardage and wearing down the defense. He has transformed his body over the past year, making him one of the fastest-rising recruits of the class.

Invited to the All-American Bowl as one of the top players in the class, where he committed to Arizona State on a national broadcast. Consensus Top-5 overall prospect in the state of New York according to all major recruiting services. Armon is tabbed as a three-star prospect by Rivals, who ranks him as the No. 4 prospect in New York. He is the first prospect that has signed with Arizona State out of New York since at least 2000.

(TX) Kenyon Green
OL Texas A&M

SPE Elite Camp 2x top OL award winner. Has started all nine games at left guard, logging 628 offensive snaps. Kenyon helped clear the way for Isaiah Spiller's fifth career 100-yard rushing game in the season-opening win over Vanderbilt. He held the line and allowed the Aggies to tally 450 yards of total offense at Alabama. He helped the Aggie rack up 543 yards of offense in the win over Florida, including 205 on the ground. Kenyon protected QB Kellen Mond and did not allow a sack for the third straight game while also only giving up one tackle for loss on the final play of the game at Mississippi State . He helped the Aggies tally 530 yards of total offense in the dominating 48-3 win at South Carolina, including 264 on the ground . He helped pave the way for Isaiah Spiller's 141 rushing yard performance in the win over LSU . Kenyon rolled over the Tiger defense for a season-high 313 yards rushing in the victory at Auburn . He contributed to a 497 total offensive yard performance in the win at Tennessee . As a unit, was named a finalist for the Joe Moore Award, named a semifinalist for the Outland Trophy, and earned second-team AP All-American and All-SEC honors . Kenyon played under Craig Stump at Atascocita High School and was an Under Armor All-American & Army All-American. Named to Dave Campbell's Texas Football Tops in Texas First Team and the Houston area UIL Offensive Player of the Year.

(CA) Jaden Navarrette
LB Oregon

Jaden came to SPE Elite Camp 2x's. He came down to Louisiana and below all the way up after a dominant performance. He was MVP runner up after playing WR and DL 1v1's. Four-star prospect by ESPN Rivals and in the 247Sports composite ranking. He was rated as a top-20 athlete in the nation by ESPN (No. 17) and Rivals (No. 7)   Ranked No. 254 in the ESPN300 as the No. 1 athlete in California and the No. 20 prospect in the state. Finished No. 303 overall and the No. 13 athlete in the class in the 247Sports composite ranking. Also a top-30 recruit in California by Rivals (No. 29) and the No. 2 athlete in the state. PrepStar Top 300 All-American ranked No. 236 nationally . A three-year letterman at Norco High School, he caught 28 passes for 565 yards and seven touchdowns and finished with 172 receiving yards and three touchdowns in a season-opening win over Williams Field High School. He recorded three tackles for loss and 1.5 sacks while forcing a fumble and making 16 tackles defensively. Jaden was named first-team All-Big VIII League on offense as a junior. He hauled in 37 receptions for 670 yards and seven touchdowns, averaging 18.1 yards per catch and recorded four sacks and 18 tackles while catching one touchdown pass as a sophomore. Had three sacks and five tackles in a win over Los Alamitos in the opening round of the CIF playoffs.

(IL) Jalen Grant
OL Bowling Green

Mr. Grant came to SPE Elite National Camp with no offers out of (IL). He put on a monster performance playing all the offensive line positions at the camp against some of the best players in the country and walked way as the 1st time ever MVP award winner by an offensive lineman. A 2019 graduate of Mount Carmel High School, he was a letterman for head coach Jordan Lynch. Jalen was named a team captain and received the Lawless Award in 2019 which is given to the most outstanding senior in the Chicago Catholic League conference . He played both offense and defense in high school and also participated in wrestling.

His freshman year at Bowling Green ,he played in all five games, starting the final three games at left guard. Jalen was part of an offensive line unit that helped the team rank among the top 50 teams in the country in rushing offense, fewest sacks allowed, and yards per completion, as well as turnovers lost.

(LA) Jacobian Guillory
DL LSU

Jacobian played at Alexandria Senior High School in Alexandria, Louisiana. He came to SPE Elite Camp 2x's and was the top DL at the camp each year. He came to the camp with no offers and ended up picking up 10 after the camp the next few moths after that. He participated in the 2020 All-American Bowl and was the most dominant force on the defensive side of the ball. Three-sport standout in football, powerlifting and track and field. Two-time state champion as a powerlifter and is a state champion in the shot put. He was rated a four-star defensive tackle by 247Sports, ESPN and Rivals. Rivals ranks him the fifth-best prospect in Louisiana and the ninth-best defensive tackle and 247Sports ranks him as the No. 6 overall prospect in the state. Tallied 38 tackles, including 10 solo in his freshman year. Helped his squad to the second round of the state playoffs in 2019. Has cleared 740 pounds in the squat, 370 pounds in the bench and 625 pounds in the deadlift. As a senior, had 76 tackles, 57 solo tackles, 27 tackles for loss, seven sacks, two forced fumbles.

(TX) Eric Mixon Jr.
LB EKU

Eric garnered first team all-district honors as a linebacker his senior season at Aldine MacArthur High School. He recorded 110 tackles, five pass break-ups, four quarterback hurries, two fumble recoveries and one forced fumble as a senior in 2019 and was team MVP as a junior after recording 117 tackles, 10 sacks, eight pass break-ups, six forced fumbles and one interception. He had 78 tackles, four sacks and three fumble recoveries his sophomore season and also had an offer from Tennessee-Martin and chose EKU because "the warmhearted welcome they provided and because coach Wells and his staff believed in me".

(LA Kyle Wickersham
QB Richmond

Two-year starter at Archbishop Rummel in Louisiana. He led his team to a 22-2 record as a starter, including a Division I 5A State Championship as a junior with a perfect 13-0 record. Ranked No. 10 in the country as a team his junior season. Rated as the No. 1 overall quarterback in this year's recruiting class in Louisiana. Ranked as a three-star recruit by 24/7 sports. As a senior, led team to a 9-2 record and a state playoff appearance. Named Player of the Week by WGNO and was named NOLA High School QBs of the Week for the 2nd time after passing for 306 yards and four touchdowns against Holy Cross. Passed for 1,691 yards and 17 touchdowns on 137-of-231 passing as a junior in his state championship season. Rushed for 199 yards and four scores that season. Father Jeff Wickersham passed for almost 7,000 yards at LSU.

(CA) Jaylin Davies
DB Oregon

This young man was one of the top DB at the camp. He is a consensus four-star recruit and top-18 cornerback nationally by Rivals (No. 6), ESPN (No. 10) the 247 composite (No. 10) and 247Sports (No. 18). Rated in the top 200 nationally overall by Rivals (No. 104), the 247 composite (No. 141) and ESPN (No. 156). Consensus top-20 player from California by Rivals (No. 8), the 247 composite (No. 13), ESPN (No. 14) and 247Sports (No. 20). Jaylin is a top four corner out of California by Rivals (No. 2), ESPN (No. 2), the 247 composite (No. 3) and 247Sports (No. 4). Named to the PrepStar Top 150 Dream Team as the magazine's No. 82 player overall. Selected to play in the 2021 Under Armour All-American Game. Named to the first-team MaxPreps 2020 Preseason High School All-American Football Team. Named to 2020 Preseason California All-State High School Football First Team by MaxPreps As a junior, named to the first-team MaxPreps 2019 Football Junior All-American Team and the MaxPreps California All-State Football First Team.

(CA) Cristian Dixon WR Michigan

Attended Mater Dei High School (2021) coached by Bruce Rollinson. He had his senior season postponed due to the COVID-19 pandemic. He hauled in 35 receptions for 611 yards and six TDs as a junior at Mater Dei. He caught 42 passes for 862 and nine touchdowns as a sophomore at Pomona Diamond Ranch. Earned a 247Sports Composite ranking of four stars; rated as the No. 222 overall player nationally, the No. 39 wide receiver in the country and the 22nd-best recruit in the state of California. Named a three-star prospect by 247Sports; the No. 61 prospect in California and the 105th-best wide receiver recruit in the nation. ESPN300 member as the nation's 140th overall recruit; rated as a four-star prospect by ESPN, the No. 25 wide receiver prospect and the 13th-best recruit in the state of California. Rivals.com four-star prospect; nation's 201st overall recruit, the No. 35 wide receiver prospect in the nation and the No. 17 player in California.

(CA) Rob Regan
DB ASU

Lockdown defensive back prospect who can eliminate the opponent's top playmaker. Wrecks an offensive game plan with his ability to shut down half of the field. Thrives in both man-to-man and zone coverage thanks to his instincts and diverse skill set. Tracks the ball in the air extremely well and has the hands to come down with interceptions in traffic. Utilizes his hands and footwork at the line of scrimmage to gain a positioning advantage and prevent the receiver from running the route. Went head-to-head with some of the top receivers in the country on the California High School footballs scene. Consensus three-star prospect according to all three major recruiting services. He left his mark at Orange Lutheran thanks to a standout junior season, finishing with 43 tackles, 20 pass deflections, and three interceptions in 11 games. He added a tackle for loss and fumble recovery as an All-Trinity Football League performer.

(LA) Sheldon Jones WR UTSA

Jones was the top WR at the SPE Elite National Camp. He appeared in all 12 games of his sophomore year of college and drew 10 starts, and caught 31 passes for 259 yards. Named to the Louisiana Nifty 50 and The Times-Picayune All-Metro team following his senior season at Warren Easton HS tallied 55 receptions for 840 yards and eight touchdowns in his final prep campaign. He helped the team to the Class 4A semifinals as a junior and caught 74 passes for 1,379 yards and 10 touchdowns in 2016.

(LA) Trey Palmer
WR LSU

Dynamic receiver who also doubles as a punt returner for the Tigers. Trey is capable of making a big play anytime he's on the field with exceptional quickness with great hands. He has the ability to stop on a dime and reverse field.

Trey will be a key component in LSU's wide receiver rotation in 2020. He played in nine games as a true freshman in 2019. He caught one pass for six yards and returned a punt for a 54-yard touchdown against Northwestern State.

Trey is one of the top players in Louisiana for the Class of 2019. He piled up 1,008 yards with nine touchdowns on 39 receptions as a senior in 2018. Averaged 25.8 yards per catch as a senior. He led his team to the Louisiana Class 1A State Championship Game 40-21, to clinch the state title . He also compiled 195 tackles, eight tackles for loss, one sack and one interception as a safety.

(CA) Faaeanuu Pepe
OL Rice

Pepe came to SPE Elite National Camp twice and got to take unofficial visits to Rice and ended up getting offered and found a home there. One of the anchors of the Lancers offensive line for coach JP Presley in the Trinity League, Pepe was the first of the 2021 class to commit to Rice. He is the current Owls wide receiver. Orange Lutheran saw its season delayed due to the pandemic and is tentatively slated to begin in January and he is the nephew of four-time Super Bowl champion Jesse Sapolu (49ers).

(LA) Marquese Albert
RB Nicholls St.

Was the top RB at the camp and ran a 4.3 at the camp. Marquese also was MVP runner up. He was a four-year letter winner at nationally-ranked John Curtis Christian and ran for 887 yards and eight touchdowns as a junior, including five 100-yard games. He led John Curtis to Catholic League title and appearance in the state semifinals. He returned two kickoffs for touchdowns in his career and missed majority of senior season with injury. He is rated by 247Sports as a three-star prospect and the No. 29 all-purpose back in the country in the class of 2018 and was the highest-ranked all-purpose back to sign with an FCS school.

(MS) Urriah Shephard
RB Ole Miss.

Was the top QB at the SPE Elite Camp. Played for coach Ty Hardin at Houston in Mississippi. He helped guide the Hilltoppers to a 9-4 overall record and the third round of the Class 3A state playoffs last season totaled 3,348 combined yards as a senior completed 72-of-164 attempts for 1,493 yards and nine touchdowns and had a career-long 88-yard completion vs. Itawamba Agricultural. He rushed for 1,855 yards and 25 touchdowns on 199 carries rushed for six touchdowns in a win against M.S. Palmer in 2017. He also compiled 58 total tackles, three interceptions, two sacks and one fumble recovery. He was part of four playoff teams at Houston four-time all-region and three-time all-area and all-state selection named Class 3A Offensive MVP. Off the field, he was named to student council and was a member of Fellowship of Christian Athletes.

(LA) Josh Clarke
LB Northwestern St.

Josh was the top linebacker at the SPE Elite Camp. He spent two years at Ole Miss and one at Holmes Community College. He was redshirted in 2017 at Ole Miss and played in four games as a redshirt freshman, making two tackles played one game at Holmes, making one tackle. Josh was a four-star recruit, according to ESPN, ranking as the No. 287 prospect nationally, Louisiana's No. 12 overall recruit and the No. 18 overall linebacker nationally three-star recruit as named by Scout and Rivals.com. Scout ranked him No. 2 outside linebacker in Louisiana . He played in the 2017 and had 118 tackles (10 for loss), six sacks, three forced fumbles and an interception as a senior at Riverdale collected 149 tackles, 18 sacks, six forced fumbles and six interceptions as a junior. He played for coach Nick Brumfield.

(LA) Quinton "Pig" Cage
DB Nicholls St.

Named Louisiana Sports Writers 5A All-State First Team and Max Preps Second Team. He was a two-time New Orleans Advocate All-Metro selection and two-time all-district. Quinton finished his senior season with 124 tackles, 19 tackles for loss, six sacks and four forced fumbles. He helped the Raiders to a 13-0 record and a state title in his senior campaign.

He also had seven sacks and four forced fumbles. In 2018, he was rated as a three-star recruit by 247 Sports and two-star by Rivals, ranked No. 42 on Dandy Don's Top 100 and also ran track, wrestled, played basketball, and was a member of the fishing team for the Raiders.

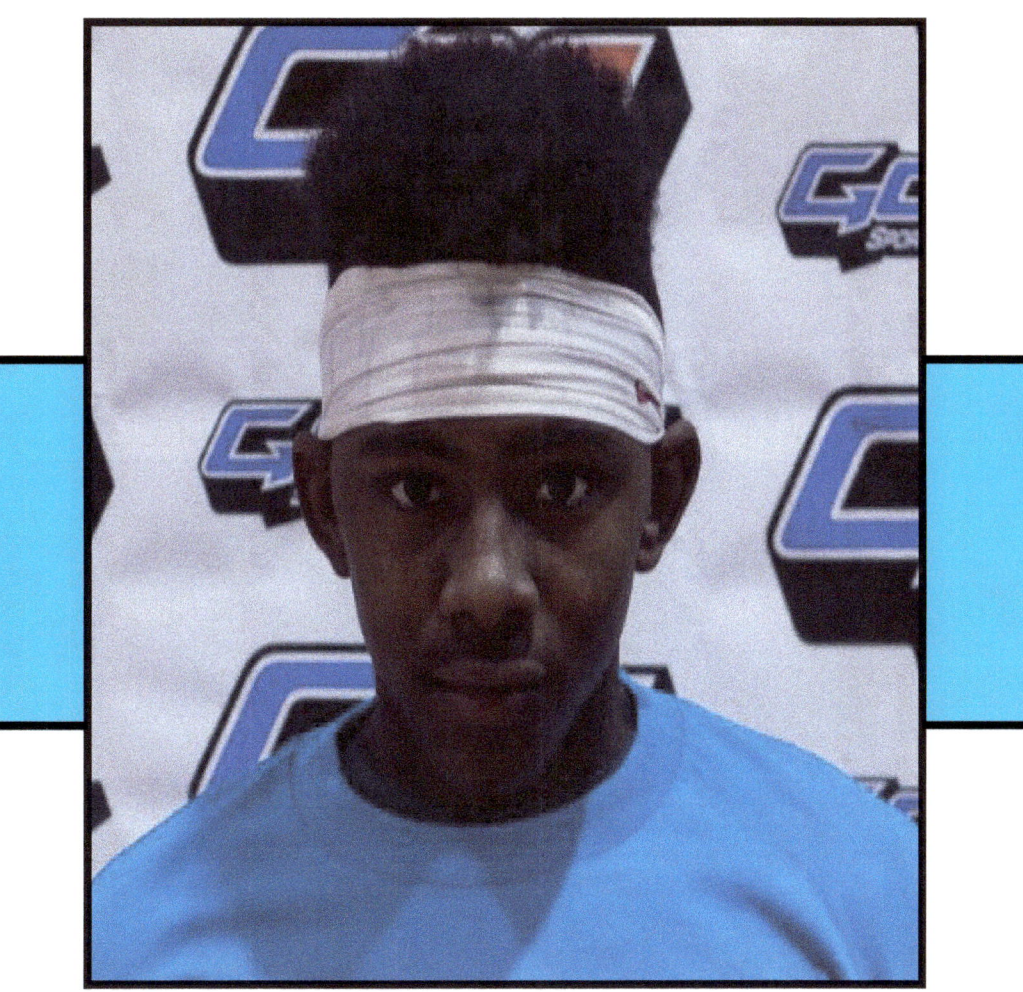

(CA) Jordan Washington
(DB) Montana Tech

Jordan Washington has a unique story through the SPE Elite Camp journey. He went to SPE Camp as an unknown player. He struggled a majority of the day but that didn't stop him from jumping up and going against the best players. He was not concerned with getting beat on plays, or how he looked to others. His main focus was getting better .

"SPE Elite Camp was a great learning experience for me, I was able to see where I was at as a player and how much better I need to be to earn a scholarship," Jordan stated.

That's what he did. He went back and worked out with different people in order to get better. He earned a chance to play college football at Montana Tech University and played in all 10 games. He recorded 18 total tackles and 3 pass breakups in 2019. He was a redshirt freshman. In high school he attended high school at Cathedral HS and voted best defensive back. Jordan finished first in 100m dash in 10.9 seconds.

(TX) Corey Anzaldua
(LB) SAGU

Corey Anzaldua committed to Southwestern Assemblies of God University [SAGU]. He came to SPE Elite National Camp 2 years in a row and he didn't let his size be a reason to not dream.

"The SPE Elite National Camp seemed like a camp where I could compete at a high level versus some of the top players in the country," Corey stated.

SAGU was a good fit academically and when they offered him a spot on the football team, Anzaldua was convinced that was were he needed to be. Anzaldua cited his dad, Isaac Anzaldua, as a big factor in signing for college football.